THE MOUNTAIN

THE MOUNTAIN

WRITTEN AND ILLUSTRATED
BY
PETER PARNALL

DOUBLEDAY & COMPANY, INC.
GARDEN CITY, NEW YORK

Library of Congress Catalog Card Number 72-145751
Copyright © 1971 by Peter Parnall
All rights reserved
Printed in the United States of America
9 8 7 6 5 4 3 2

DEDICATED TO THE CREATURES THAT LIVED THERE

This is the mountain that stood in the West.

These are the flowers that grew there.

These are the moles that

smelled the flowers

that grew on the mountain that stood in the West.

These are the birds that lived in the trees

that sheltered the deer
that lived in the forest

that grew on the mountain
that stood in the West.

These are the
people

who loved the mountain and wanted to keep it

...just

...it was.

...the way

So, Congress passed a law
making the mountain a NATIONAL PARK

and
a road
was built.

This is a flower...trying to grow
on the mountain that stood in the West.

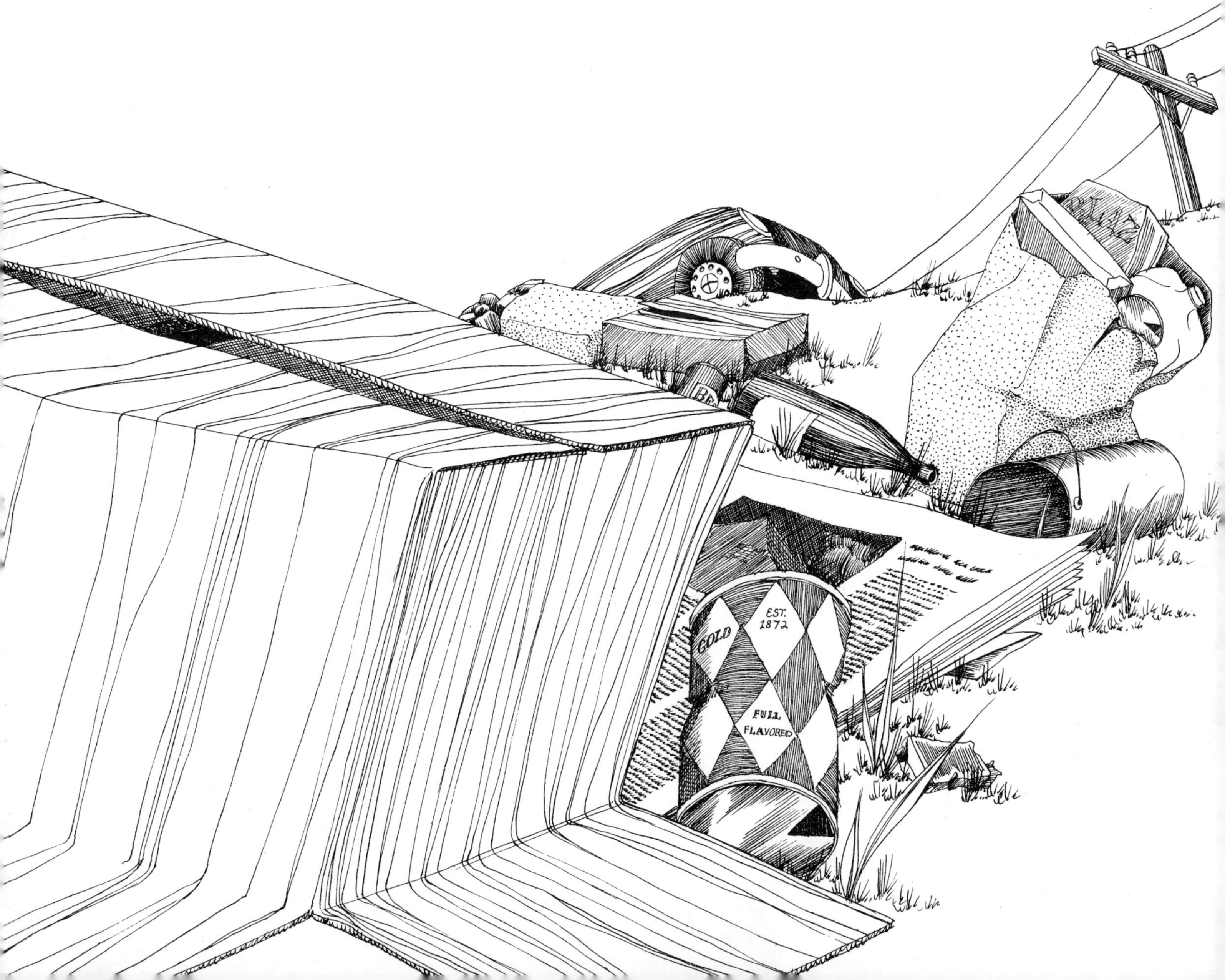
GOLD
EST.
1872
FULL
FLAVORED

Peter Parnall was born in Syracuse, New York, and attended Cornell University and Pratt Institute. Mr. Parnall has been an art director for a small magazine, has founded and run his own magazine, and for ten years was a free-lance advertising designer. Some years ago he moved to a country farm and began devoting his full time to children's books. Since then he has illustrated many books, including *The Inspector, The Dog's Book of Bugs,* and *A Beastly Circus* and has won a number of awards from the American Institute of Graphic Arts and the Society of Illustrators, as well as having had several books chosen for The New York *Times* annual Best Illustrated Books list. Currently Mr. Parnall teaches design at Lafayette College. He and his wife and son live in Milford, New Jersey, where in his spare time he pursues such hobbies as training horses, gun engraving, and breeding fighting chickens.

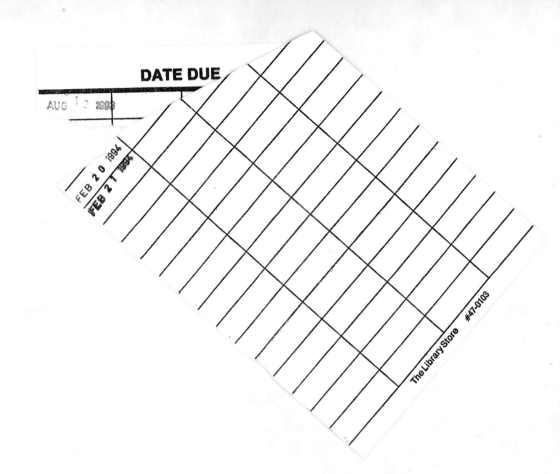